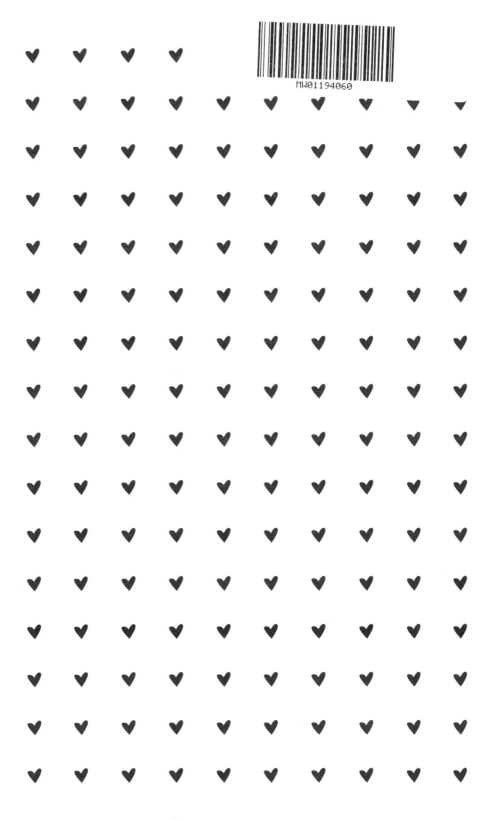

To

From

Occasion

chance meetings that tied knot

that the

Finding Love
When Least Expected

by

JAN NEWMAN

Published by
The Newman Group, Ltd.
Burlingame, CA 94010

Design and Illustration by Jennifer Keith

Library of Congress
Cataloging-in-Publication Data
Newman, Jan

Chance Meetings That Tied The Knot
ISBN 0-9773853-0-2
9780977385300

First Edition

Dedication

This book is dedicated to Bob,
my chance meeting and husband,
for being my guiding light
and giving me the enthusiastic
encouragement needed to
make this book a reality.

Acknowledgments

Over the years I have asked this question of countless couples: "How did you two meet?" I owe a BIG thank you to all who have shared their stories with me and to those who will share their stories with me in the future.

A special thank you to my illustrator Jennifer Keith who translated the stories into visual sound bites, my editor Valery Fahey for tightening my prose, my readers Jill Chozen, Judy Einzig, Lisa Grotts, Ronnie Harlan, Joyce Hoffspiegel, Beth Izmirian, Jennifer Saranow and Jeanie Schram for their support and critique, and my teacher Lisa Alpine for words of wisdom mixed with actionable advice.

Additional thanks are extended to all readers of this book who took a chance on *Chance Meetings*...may you find love.

Preface

I know first hand that a chance meeting can change a life. As a freshman in college, my last minute decision to attend the Chancellor's Tea brought me face-to-face with the man I would marry. It was love at first sight. Over the last thirty-plus years of married bliss, I've uncovered hundreds of "chance meetings." Some are simple stories about meeting one's soulmate at the post office, ATM or by the copier machine at work. Other stories have more complex serendipitous settings.

Chance Meetings That Tied the Knot is based on true stories about people from every background, age and setting. Each story is an example of a chance meeting culminating with finding true and enduring love. These stories illustrate that circumstance, choice, and personal awareness are key in producing such chance meetings. At the core of this book is a new heightened awareness that in our everyday lives, love is waiting. Use these stories to uplift your spirit, or guide you toward the path of love.

This book would not have been possible without the many people who shared their personal stories. It is my greatest hope that readers of this book will be transported to the magical place of love instilled by these wonderful chance meetings.

TABLE OF CONTENTS

Table of Contents

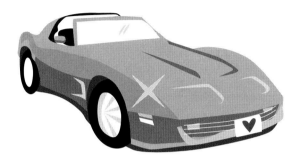

MET BY ACCIDENT
ALEXANDRA'S STORY

I was 24, with blue eyes and blond hair. I had that L.A. "Valley Girl" look. Unfortunately, I recently broke up with a guy I'd been dating for a while. It was one of those relationships that you thought was going to go somewhere but just never was able to pick up enough speed to get airborne. Oh well, I decided to cut my losses and moved back home to Palo Alto from Southern California where I had gone to college at USC.

Shortly after my move back home, I was selected for a Neiman Marcus buyer-training program and started to make new friends at work. One of my friends was Jennifer, a sales associate. I remember counseling her on ending some of her "bad girl" habits.

"You know, Jennifer, it really isn't safe to drive if you've been drinking," I stated.

Jennifer confided in me that she often went drinking at a local bar after work and then dared herself to drive home while intoxicated.

I found this appalling and said firmly, "Anytime, day or night, when you've been drinking call me."

Fast-forward two days. It was now 2:00 A.M. and I was tucked snuggly in bed and sound asleep. The telephone was ringing.

Was I having a dream? Who was calling me at this ungodly hour? I reached for the phone. Jennifer was on the other end of the receiver laughing and bubbling into the phone, "I had too much to drink and you said to call."

I flung off the covers and quickly wiped the sleep from my eyes. I had on pajama bottoms and a tank top. To this I added a sweatshirt for warmth and my pink fuzzy slippers, the kind that looked like a family of trolls who hadn't combed their hair in years. Off I went to save Jenny.

The bar was about 15 minutes from my apartment. Fortunately, Jennifer lived close to me so I figured this total good deed would take no more than 30 minutes.

I drove a silver SUV with big black bars on the front grill, the kind for pushing cows around. Why did I drive this vehicle? Because it was what all blond USC co-eds drove!

I made it into the car and began my trip to the bar. I was so sleepy that I overshot the street I needed to turn on. Because it was one-way, I had to go around the block to access the street again. I was at a four-way intersection and the light was yellow. I thought to myself *let's get this over*, and crossed the intersection knowing that caution would normally be my rule. I made a very wide right turn. Bang...I felt the instant jolt and the impact of a crash.

"Are you kidding me? This did not just happen," was all I could say to the young man climbing out of the silver Corvette I had just plowed into.

I just kept repeating, "I am so sorry. I am so sorry." All he wanted to do was to call the police. I calmed down enough and persuaded him not to call the police and instead just take my name and insurance information. I really didn't want them involved.

We drove our vehicles to the side of the road in order to avoid a scene. My proof of insurance card had both my name and my dad's on it since I was on his insurance policy. I think Craig the Corvette owner thought

I was married when he took this information.

I had totally forgotten what I was wearing — pajama bottoms, sweatshirt, and pink fuzzy slippers and asked him, "Why don't I buy you a drink?" I felt he might need one after the mess I made of his car.

"No thanks," Craig replied, visibly embarrassed by my outfit.

Fortunately we could both drive our cars away from the accident scene. He left and I continued down the block to rescue Jennifer from the bar. I just couldn't believe what had happened. One minute I was innocently sleeping, and the next I was in a fender bender.

The following day I called Craig at work to again say, "I am so sorry." I also asked him to send me his insurance estimates so I could have his car repaired.

Craig was a software engineer and very computer literate. I was barely up to sending e-mail. Within a few days I started receiving regular e-mail and attachments from Craig. Not realizing what these attachments contained, I deleted them thinking they may cause a computer virus.

I later learned the attachments to the e-mails I was deleting included the estimates for his car repairs.

Since I wasn't great with e-mail, Craig and I developed a wonderful phone dialogue. We would talk aimlessly for hours about absolutely nothing. We never saw each other in person. I started to think I had a crush on him. *What was I thinking?*

It was now the night of my birthday. A group of my girlfriends gave a beautiful surprise party for me the night before the actual date, and on the day, Jill, a good friend, agreed to go to the local club with me. I had thought about Craig all day and decided I wanted to see him. I figured that my birthday was a good enough reason for him to have a drink with me. After reaching Craig on the phone and encouraging him to come to the club, I nonchalantly asked what he would be wearing.

Craig replied, "Jeans, a white shirt and a red cap," the preferred outfit of most guys at the club.

I hope I'll recognize him, I thought.

I gave Craig's description to the club bouncer and eagerly waited for him at the bar. When Craig entered the club I immediately knew who he was by his preferred outfit.

I don't know what made me do the next thing but I immediately went over to him and gave him a big hug in public. At that moment our worlds collided a second time. I couldn't let go. I never wanted to let go. I felt safe in his embrace. Time stood still. I felt my whole world turn upside down.

Craig handed the hard copy of the estimates to a friend he saw in the crowd who promptly tore them up like pieces of confetti. We started to throw the torn-up estimates into the air as a sign of celebration.

A month later we were talking marriage. We were officially engaged on New Years Day six months after that, and ultimately tied the knot 18 months later.

At our engagement party Craig brought the infamous damaged bumper from the Corvette as proof of our accidental encounter!

♥

Alexandra's Lesson

Trust your gut. Intuition is most often right!

THE RED BIKINI
GLADYS'S STORY

About 15 years after I was married, almost to the day, my husband asked for a divorce. Our marriage seemed normal to me. We both had interesting but demanding jobs: he was a pilot and I, a molecular biologist. Our family life revolved around our careers, helping our aging parents, travel and our mutual hobbies of antique cars and sports. Since we were first married, our respective careers meant a lot to both of us. Through hard work, perseverance and a little luck, we were finally experiencing success in our jobs and paychecks that made life comfortable.

Being a pilot did have some perks. My husband had a world pass for both of us that allowed travel anywhere at anytime. We tried to make the most of this benefit and visited many far-off and exotic places, as well as major world destinations. Paris, London, Tokyo, Guatemala, Barbados, Jamaica, Brussels and Germany were memories in our photo album.

Looking back on our marriage, I realized that my husband wanted a stay-at-home wife: a woman who was totally involved in the domestic arts, who would greet him with a clean house and a warm dinner. My personal mantra was different. I was a woman who had a PhD in biochemistry and finished a four-year fellowship in molecular biology. I was not going to chuck it all and stay at home. I had a great opportunity to help benefit science and mankind. My husband seemed a little selfish.

We separated amicably in the spring. There were no fits of anger, tantrums, or verbal abuse. We had gradually grown apart rather than together. Our marriage was like a houseplant that at first was placed in a sunny spot and watered regularly, but then, was moved to a dark corner, forgotten, only to slowly wither away.

The first year of separation was difficult. I buried myself in research work and teaching responsibilities as an assistant professor at the New York Medical College. By the end of the next winter I was desperate for a vacation. I hadn't gone anywhere in almost a year. My blood needed a warm weather fix and my complexion had suffered from lack of sun. My entire physical state was slowly going into withdrawal. In two weeks I would have a cherished week of vacation.

I closed my eyes and imagined the heat of the sun, breathing new life into my paled winter skin. I took a risk.

"Does that travel pass in my name still work?" I inquired as I left a message on my ex-husband's answering machine. "If the answer is yes, would you please book me a flight, somewhere warm with a beach. How about Tahiti? My winter break is from February16-23."

I had never been to the South Pacific. Just thinking about the prospect of getting away started to lift my spirits. A few days later, I received a message on my answering machine.

"The pass is still good but I can't get you to Tahiti. Gosh, Gladys, you need to plan a trip like that farther out than two weeks. Hey, I booked you to Kauai instead. It should be warm and there's a beach."

It was 15 degrees outside. The wind was blowing fiercely and at two in the afternoon it looked like the middle of night. The vacation news immediately lightened my spirit and propelled me into action. It was only a matter of days until I would be in paradise.

The next ten days were busy from morning 'till night. I had to finish my teaching duties, write, give, and grade a midterm exam and get my warm weather gear together.

I prided myself on packing light. Besides, how much stuff did you really need if all you planned to do was camp out on a chaise lounge for a week? My small carryon had enough room for everything. This was much better than schlepping a big suitcase and dealing with baggage claim.

I was looking for my white cotton beach cover-up when I spied an almost forgotten, never worn purchase. In a very weak moment two summers before, I dared myself to buy a red bikini at the swim store near Jones Beach. *Hawaii will be the perfect place to wear this fashion statement.*

My flight from New York to L.A. was uneventful. I arranged a layover to spend the evening with my former in-laws with whom I had maintained an excellent relationship. I was so tired that when I went to bed at their house that night, I forgot to set an alarm. You guessed it. I missed my flight.

After waiting at the L.A. airport for an extra four hours, I was finally airborne. My ex told me that when I arrived in Kauai, a representative with a van would take me to the resort. He had made all the arrangements for me. It was only when I landed that I looked at the name of the place I would call home for the next week. It was called Club Med. I had never heard of it. As long as it had a beach I'd be happy.

Just as promised, a young man wearing flip-flops, shorts and a Hawaiian shirt sporting hula girls met me outside the baggage claim area. It was a thirty-minute ride to the resort from the airport. Upon arriving, I went to the check-in desk and discovered I would be sharing a room with another woman. All the rooms at Club Med were for two people. No singles were allowed.

At first I was miffed with this revelation, but then resigned myself to fate, knowing I planned to spend as little time as possible in my room. *How could my ex put me up in a place like this? No single rooms? What was he thinking?*

After unpacking my things, my first line of duty was to find a chaise lounge under a palm tree so I would have a little natural shade. Wearing my red bikini, I fit in perfectly with the other guests at the resort. Most of the guests I observed to be between 20 and 50. No families with kids were in view. This was an adult only resort.

I walked past several different pool areas, a bar that was reconstructed from an old sailboat and then spotted a semi-secluded place overlooking the deep blue Pacific. I spied six white chaises. Four were already occupied by two men and two women deeply engrossed in their novels. I quietly slid into one of the two vacant lounge chairs. In my beach bag I found my sunscreen, tinted reading glasses, and the half-finished mystery I started when my plane left New York. I performed the necessary rituals prior to sunbathing and began to read. *I had found paradise!*

About 15 minutes into my book a cute man clad in shorts and a Club Med logo T-shirt stopped by the six chairs. "Hope everyone is having fun today! Can I get anyone a drink? We've got a great rum fruit punch, piña coladas, ice tea, and lemonade. What can I get you?"

"I'll have an ice tea with lemon. Thanks for asking," I replied.

The man next to me ordered four rum and cokes and while looking at me inquisitively he added, "Why don't you bring the lady in the red bikini a Long Island iced tea."

"Thanks, but no thanks," I replied. "Regular ice tea will be just fine. I'm not a big drinker especially before dinner."

Now the men and women in the four adjacent chaises were trying to engage me in conversation. I didn't want to be rude, but conversation with strangers was not what I had in mind. Politely, I introduced myself and we exchanged basic information: where we lived and how often we'd been at Club Med. They had been to Club Med five times, in my case, never.

After a few minutes of their boring banter I withdrew myself from the conversation and said, "I don't mean to be rude but I have to turn over and get my left side tan." I rolled over and that was that.

The sixth chaise lounge was now occupied by a man who was wearing a brightly patterned red and white bathing suit with coordinating shirt. *Where did he come from? I sure didn't hear him claim that chaise.*

He couldn't take his eyes off me. He was just smiling and looking at me in an amused fashion. I didn't want to turn back to the left and deal with the Club Med groupies. I looked around to see if there were any other vacant chairs but none were in sight.

I didn't say a word. I just closed my eyes and pretended to sleep. After a few minutes, I heard the guy delivering the drink order. I scooted to a more upright position, careful that my bikini top didn't slide down my chest since I had untied the straps around my neck.

The man was still looking at me and finally spoke. "Thanks for wearing the red bikini. How'd you know that red's my favorite color?" Continuing in a more confessional tone he added, "I've never been to a Club Med before. It reminds me of summer camp. I'm here alone and feel a little out of place. Any suggestions?"

There was something about the way he looked at me that was very intriguing. We discovered that we had many similar likes. Reading was a passion for both of us. We liked to swim in the ocean and ride the surf. He seemed very intelligent and we had similar liberal political views. I immediately liked him.

For the following week we were inseparable: walks on the beach, swimming in the surf, bonfires, dinner under the stars, and endless conversation. My bookmark didn't move in my mystery all week.

We were so enthralled with our companionship that I rearranged my trip back to New York through San Francisco where Larry lived. We spent three beautiful days together before I headed back home.

We began a long-distance romance. After three months, Larry asked me to move in with him. I had to wait until my divorce was final, but I accepted. Within the year, I moved across the country. A man who valued my mind and profession gave me a second chance at love. I'm so glad I wore that red bikini!

♥

Gladys's Lesson

Take a risk. A solo vacation may have a surprising ending.
And, it doesn't hurt to wear something like a red bikini!

JOB HUNTING
MELINDA'S* STORY

I was 30. Over the past few years many boyfriends and proposals had come my way. So far no one had the stuff that really turned me on – a man who could make me laugh, with decent values, at least five feet six inches tall, who wanted a family.

Disenchanted with my current accounting job, I decided to look for a new opportunity. I answered an ad for a position as controller at a small insurance company. They liked my résumé and called me for an interview. I was scheduled to meet with several key employees, including the owner of the company.

Every time I had an interview I got a little nervous. *Will I make a good impression? Do they think I'm qualified? How will they treat a woman in a job that is typically male-dominated?*

I arrived at the company feeling very confident. Immediately, I was ushered into the owner's office, and it was startled to find that the owner was a handsome young man who was about my age.

The interview started with the usual questions, nevertheless, I felt a

*First name changed.

sense of excitement. *Was it the job? What was going on? Why did I feel like a shy little girl? Was I blushing?* I had never felt this way before in the presence of a man, especially one I hardly knew. My current boyfriend certainly didn't excite me in the same way. He was more like a comfortable old shoe, predictable and not very creative. I soon realized that this man knew a heck of a lot more about me than I knew about him because his HR department had given him my résumé and references. He had done his homework!

Toward the end of the interview, I felt completely confused about the experience. One part of me thought, *thank him for the opportunity to talk about working for his company and tell him you would like to work for him.* Another part wanted to say, "This job wasn't right for me, but it was great to meet you."

Before I had a chance to contemplate either of these replies, the owner said, "I don't usually offer a prospective employee a job on the spot, but your credentials are impressive and you're a lovely lady. I've never made a decision like this before."

There was a pause. I thought I saw a bead of sweat on his brow. After a moment he continued, "Take the job – or date me. Choose one, but you can't do both. I'm not one to promote office romances!" I thought about it for a nanosecond and chose him. We were married shortly after that.

Melinda's Lesson

Sometimes your game plan needs to be adjusted to seize the moment.

TEA FOR TWO
JAN'S STORY

It was September 1968. Even though I was mature for my 18 years, I had never been away from home for more than two weeks. Everything about Wash U was so exciting – new people, new places, and new beginnings. I remember my father driving me to the campus in our family Buick which was packed to the gills. Our destination? Washington University, in St. Louis. It was requested that all freshmen be on campus several days before classes started to move into their dorm rooms, unpack and get acclimated. After my dad left to make the six-hour trip back home, I busily settled in.

Finally the big event arrived: my first day of classes, freshman year. We started at 8:30 A.M. and went until 4:00 P.M. It was a full day for sure.

Before I left that first morning, I heard a knock on my door. "Hi," said Jenny with a twang. "Great to meet you. I'm in room 322. I guess you figured out from my accent I'm from Texas. I hope we'll be friends."

I had just finished dressing and was in a hurry to leave. Jenny persisted anyway, "I was hoping you could help me out with something. The girls on our dorm floor are going to the Chancellor's Tea. It's supposed to be a great place to meet guys. All the girls had paired up so that everyone had a buddy. Call it protection, if you want. If an upperclassman hits on you, and you don't want to be with him, we're each other's excuse! I'd love to go, but I need a buddy."

This sounded reasonable, but I had read something about this event in the campus newspaper. It sounded only marginally interesting, if not a little stuffy.

Another concern was how to hold on to the memory of my high school boyfriend. We dated for two years, knowing that college was going to be the end. But to me, college men seemed so intimidating.

I first declined Jenny's offer, but she wouldn't take no for an answer. Before I knew what had happened, she had talked me into meeting her at 4:30 P.M. to walk to the tea.

I remember dressing in my green Villager suit, matching green Pappagallo flats, and green Bermuda bag. My hair was styled in a smooth pageboy, and I wore black eyeliner and white lipstick like all the other girls. When we arrived at the tea, there was a sea of upper classmen checking out the female freshmen. All the guys were dressed in blue blazers, white button-down collar shirts, and ties. Oh, so proper. They looked like they all belonged to the same fraternity. As it turned out, many did.

Everyone seemed very friendly. I soon lost Jenny to a big hunk of a guy. She didn't seem to mind it in the least. Now on my own, I immediately joined a lively conversation about the college football team. All of a sudden, I found myself talking to a really cute guy with a mustache.

I was in awe of his hair – a color something between strawberry-blond and red. Nothing out of a bottle could ever capture this hue. I thought, *Too bad it's wasted on a guy!* Out of curiosity I asked, "Where did you get that gorgeous hair?"

He replied, "My dad's was the same color when he was my age. Unfortunately, I don't remember it because he's gray and balding. I sure hope that isn't my fate!"

We introduced ourselves and started talking about our respective hometowns and families. I found out he was a junior and a member of the fraternity ZBT, which was hosting the tea event. He also had a blue Ford Galaxy convertible, a necessity for off campus dating. He seemed so nice and easy going.

Now I had a dilemma. I had promised my mother (under threat of not being allowed to attend college out-of-state) that I would only date Jewish men in college. That was the deal I agreed to in high school. I had to find out if he was Jewish. I pondered, *How could a redhead be Jewish? Just my luck. And he's so adorable. The only Jewish men I've ever seen had brown hair.* Now I was really in a pickle of a situation. I had to find out if he was "safe" to date, so that I wouldn't break the agreement with my mother.

From out of nowhere I thought of a question. "I hope it isn't too forward of me, but I'd love to go to that mall in Clayton. I've been stuck on campus since I got here two weeks ago. I need to buy a Bar Mitzvah gift for a cousin of mine. What was your favorite Bar Mitzvah gift?"

There was a slight pause, and then he responded, "I still have cuff links, book ends and a black fountain pen."

My heart skipped a beat, *Yes, he's Jewish. He's dating material. Mom would approve.* I totally forgot Jenny my buddy, as well as my high school sweetheart, and was off to the shopping mall in the convertible with the top down.

Bob immediately became my first and only college boyfriend. We felt so comfortable in each other's presence. There were no growing pains. It felt right from day one, and our relationship continued to get better with each passing day.

The rest is history. Bob is the light of my life. He is generous to a fault, sensitive and caring: the perfect mate. Our parents met two months later when both families had Thanksgiving together, which is now a long standing tradition. We found out that both sets of parents had married soon after the end of World War II in Chicago, and wouldn't you know, by the same rabbi. What a coincidence!

I'm ever so thankful that Jenny insisted I go with her to the Chancellor's Tea. I married that red headed guy four years later. That was 1972. You do the math.

Jan's Lesson

Doing something for someone else may have a surprising payback.

THE COFFEE BAR
JEANIE'S STORY

In three months I'd be 30 and my life was anything but settled. I had just finished my course work for my doctorate in the School of Education at Stanford University. Before I would be awarded my degree, I had to write my dissertation – no small task. I also recently moved from the college town of Palo Alto to San Francisco, forty-five minutes to the north. After four years of living the quiet life, I yearned for the city. I still missed my native New York, and was unsure about life in California. It seemed cheaper to try San Francisco than to move all my stuff across the country. Fortunately, I found an adorable little apartment that was within my student budget in an area called North Beach. My street housed an Italian deli, a newspaper stand, and was punctuated with little cafés.

Just before I found my *pied-à-terre*, I took a one-week trip to Acapulco with my dear friend Cathy. Cathy worked for the Hyatt Hotel chain. We shared a room so my only expense was airfare. We had a great week in the sun, and sported dark glossy tans when we returned to San

Francisco. This trip was consolation from a dear friend to ease the pain of a bad break-up a few weeks earlier. I vowed to avoid men so I could stay focused on finishing my work and move on to living what would be my real life.

Now the day of reckoning had come. Relaxed from my vacation, I was ready to start my dissertation. One minor detour remained. My car needed some work so I could safely commute to Stanford.

My appointment was for 7:00 A.M. on Monday, and they needed the car all day. On the bus ride home, I remembered a friend had insisted that I go to North Beach's most historic café for the quintessential San Francisco experience. "Hey" I rationalized, "another hour won't make a difference." I exited the bus one stop early. It was easy to find Caffee Trieste – the coffee aroma was seductive and the eclectic mix of people revealed that yuppies and hippies were alive and well in North Beach.

I went inside and found an empty seat at a round table. I took out a brown Mexican cigarette, a leftover from my recent vacation, and was immediately offered a light by a man who deposited his cappuccino next to mine.

"Hi there. I'm Richard. Have you been to Mexico recently?"

I laconically replied, "I guess my Acapulco T-shirt and my Mexican cigarettes are a dead giveaway."

Richard smiled. "Your dead giveaway is your dark tan. The only beach I know where you can get that kind of tan is in Mexico." Richard didn't want to seem too forward and explained, "Here at Caffee Trieste people share their tables. May I join you?"

Richard was trying hard to engage me. "So what are some of your favorite places in San Francisco?"

Being new to the city, I turned the question back to him, "I just moved here a week ago, so I don't have any. What are yours?"

Richard started reeling off some names then all of a sudden looked at his watch. "Just a minute. I need to make a phone call." He left the table and found the pay phone next to the entrance. In a few minutes he came back. "May I offer you a ride home? I have my car outside. I come here every morning before work for a cappuccino."

At first I hesitated, but then found my voice, "That would be very nice. It's a beautiful morning. I could walk, but, if it's not any trouble, a ride would be great."

Richard led me outside to a cute green sports car with the top down. "I thought I could take the day off from work," he said, "to show you some of the great things about the city. I can't do it this morning but I could come back for you at lunchtime. What do you say?"

I started to reflect that I really needed to begin that dissertation. I even had it on my calendar. *What a nice unpushy guy. Hummm…great coffee, gorgeous day, lunch date. What about my green and white blouse? Hey, another day won't make a difference!* "Yes!"

Noon came and soon we were whizzing across the Golden Gate Bridge to a restaurant where we could eat outdoors, next to the beach. He seemed to have an ability to discuss almost anything. He was very well read and up-to-date on current events. The afternoon raced by.

As the sun set Richard became quiet, and then he said, "I'd really like to see you again. This has been a great day."

Within the next eight weeks we got to know each other better. We discovered that we shared so many of the same interests and values – a love of music, reading, and seeing San Francisco's beautiful sights with the top down. Fifteen months later we married.

Our wedding rings are engraved inside with "love and coffee forever." Twenty-six years later, the coffee is decaf and only in the morning. The love? High octane, triple shot, extra grande.

♥

Jeanie's Lesson

It is important to take time to "smell the roses".
All work and no play makes for a very dreary day.

.

CHAMPAGNE THE DRINK OF CHOICE
LISA'S STORY

I'd recently switched jobs and was feeling my way through the protocol of my new firm. There seemed to be rules for everything. I was trying to climb the corporate ladder in sales. I was in my early 30s, learning the ropes at yet another Fortune 500 firm. A typical day included time in the office and in the field. I loved the variety this job offered. After work, I usually went to the gym or did errands before going home to slide a Lean Cuisine into the microwave.

After several weeks on the job, my sales unit agreed to meet at a bar one evening for a little socializing. I was looking forward to an evening with my work associates because it would be a different setting than a typical 9 to 5 day. It would give me a chance to get to know them on a more personal basis. Since we worked on computer issues, our discussions rarely touched on movies, restaurants, or the arts.

Upon entering the bar I was surprised to find that I was the first of my unit to arrive. I thought, *We did agree to meet tonight, at the bar, right after work, or did I get the date, time or place wrong?* Not to waste time in this setting, I tried to scope out the scene. There were a few groups of twos and one larger party of six men. I could see one of the men in this group looking at me. *Oh where were my work associates?* I decided that this visual flirtation might not be so bad, but, to my surprise, the man made no further eye contact. Now I decided that time was of the essence and every minute counted. I did not want to look like a wallflower. I started to search the bar to see what the other customers were drinking. I saw wine, a lot of beer, and, at the far end of the bar, I spied a bottle of champagne and one glass. Its owner, however, was nowhere to be seen.

My next action was totally out of character. I'm usually not a very forward person, but on this occasion, I did something radical.

I moved to the place at the bar where the lonely bottle of champagne sat. I casually asked the bartender for an extra glass and poured myself a little champagne. I thought that I would like to meet the person who was drinking champagne because it suggested a person of refinement. Champagne just said "classy" to me. Whenever I drank it, I had visual images of candlelight and romance. I guess those little bubbles worked magic on my brain.

I was contentedly sipping when a young man with dark brown hair and soft brown eyes came to claim his glass. From my perspective, he was the prince charming I had always dreamed about. He looked at me and asked, "And who is sipping my champagne?" I introduced myself and blushed when he said that I was the perfect accompaniment to his bubbly beverage. It was love at first sight. Wedding bells followed within the year!

♥

Lisa's Lesson

When original plans seem not to work, don't give up.
Unorthodox behavior may bring excitement and joy. Step into your dreams.

A SOLO DATE BRINGS GOOD LUCK WITH A MATE
JOYCE'S STORY

I was a clinical psychologist from New Jersey, divorced and unattached, spending the week of my 45th birthday checking out colleges in Arizona with my 17-year-old son Greg. From the beginning of our trip, I sensed that some firmly held part of me was open for change. In Scottsdale we discovered that our reserved hotel was overbooked and that we had been transferred instead to a new luxurious world-class resort. We had been ushered into a life of elegance and privilege.

The first morning of our stay, I recalled glancing at the other hotel guests, particularly at couples, as Greg and I lingered over breakfast discussing colleges at the posh outdoor Mediterranean café. Basking in the glorious February sun, I recalled thinking *I could live this Western lifestyle, with February birthdays by the pool.* Then it occurred to me that *I should be with a man like that* (selecting a somewhat older, distinguished looking man sitting nearby), *a man who could help provide this for me.* I remembered assessing my attributes, weighing my assets and concluding that I was as desirable as the cared-for women securely coupled with what I assumed to be businessmen husbands.

Shocked and a bit ashamed of these thoughts I realized that my long-standing assumptions and attitudes about my relationship with men were in flux. Until that moment I had never considered wealth, power or lifestyle as necessary criteria for a man in my life. I had come of age during the height of the women's liberation movement. Between two marriages I had earned my doctorate, raised two children, been an academic and clinical psychologist and felt pretty self-satisfied. Moreover, I was financially independent, enjoying an upper middle-class life. I had grown up following the credo, "Become the man you always wanted to marry." Men were to be enjoyed and loved, but not depended upon financially. I was attracted to handsome, warm, intellectual and artistic men, but generally not to businessmen at all.

Amused by my momentary departure from sanity, I dismissed my free associations as temporary lapses from reality, vacation-induced fantasies that did not represent my true inner self.

Following our Arizona college tours, Greg and I decided to take a side trip to Las Vegas. Neither of us had visited the town before. We had two vacation days remaining until we headed home to winter in New Jersey. Unknowingly, we drove into town during one of its busiest weekends. Celebrities, sports fans and a collection of intriguing characters had gathered at the Hilton for the Bruno-Tyson boxing match, the same day as my birthday.

Feeling self-indulgent following the pampering at our last resort and reminding myself that it was my birthday, I splurged on a manicure, new outfit and dinner with Greg at the Hilton that evening. Although I had no interest in prizefighting, I had to admit I was fascinated by the drama and intensity of the scene played out in the hotel lobby. The pre-fight crowd consisted of paparazzi, glamorous men and women, swaggering gangster types, and men in cowboy boots and casual western attire who seemed qualitatively different in demeanor from men I had ever encountered. I felt as if I was in the "Star Wars" bar scene, except this mix of people seemed appealing, not bizarre.

An ardent people-watcher, I had expected that Greg and I would wander around the hotel after dinner. However, after dessert, Greg informed me he had plans to get together with a girl he had met that day. I knew it wasn't cool for a 17-year-old guy to be hanging out with his mom on a Saturday night in Vegas so I encouraged him to have a good time. Of course, now I was left on my own! It was only ten o'clock and my first instinct was to head back to our hotel room and read a good book. I definitely didn't feel comfortable exploring Las Vegas by myself. Fortunately, my inner therapist voice immediately vetoed my cowardly plans for withdrawal. *What would you advise your women clients?* I knew the answer but I was resisting independent action. *This is an exciting place and you don't feel like going to your room at this hour. Stop acting like an abandoned child.*

Listening to my own counsel, I walked into the hotel casino just as the fight crowd was exiting the big event. Tyson had scored a knockout in an early round and the ticket holders clearly wanted more action. With press cameras flashing, and a buzz of excitement in the air, clusters of men and women were elbowing their way into an adjacent cocktail lounge. Determined to act like my idealized version of an adult woman, I followed the crowd, sat in a darkly lit banquette and ordered a diet coke. My self-consciousness dimmed as a celebrity guest commandeered the stage and started singing to his appreciative pals. The band began to play and other celebrities vied for their turn to perform. This was turning into a spectacular evening. I was proud that I had taken myself out on a date. Amazingly, I started to feel relaxed and pleased with my actions. *No one knew me here and it didn't matter if I was alone*. At that moment a man politely asked me to dance. This guy was attractive, broad-shouldered, tall and clearly self-assured. I like to dance and figured I had nothing to lose. I accepted his invitation, then I spent the next three hours talking to him in the lounge.

Dave was not someone I could quickly categorize. He had curly dark hair streaked with gray (older signals than I preferred) and he sported a mustache that covered his otherwise handsome features. He was self-assured and calm yet dominant and take-charge in a manner that might have turned me off in the past. He lived in California's Central Valley (an agricultural center, not an alluring geographical area for me) and was newly separated (e.g., in transition). He'd flown his own plane to attend the fight with his son. He actually liked boxing! *What kind of guy is this?*

Dave was a businessman (a no-no) and he was initially vague describing a variety of business involvements. He seemed intelligent, kind and masculine. He also had too much to drink and tried to kiss me (*Who does he think he is?*).

Sixteen months later Dave and I were married. He shaved his mustache. We've been together for fourteen years and with him I've come to experience a deep and enduring love. After I relocated to California, we moved to Pebble Beach.

Dave's a very successful entrepreneur (not an intellectual or artist) and an accomplished sailor, pilot, skier, and car-collector. He has introduced me to a world and experiences I would never have found on my own. He's also the most competent and decent man I've ever met. And yes, I like depending on him, at least partially, for this wonderful life style, and I love birthdays by the pool!

♥

Joyce's Lesson

Act on the advice you give to others.

FIRST-CLASS *IS* BETTER THAN COACH
SUSAN'S STORY

Los Angeles was my home, but I often traveled to San Francisco on business. It's a short flight – just under an hour. There were lots of flights throughout the day. I think it's one of the most popular airline routes in the state. So when I tried to make a reservation to fly to San Francisco on the first Monday in May, I was surprised to learn that all of the coach seats were sold. There were a few first-class seats available, but they were much more expensive.

I was a freelancer, and always trying to watch expenses. Traveling on an airplane was like traveling on a bus: you'll get to your destination at the same time no matter where you park your body, first-class or coach. With that philosophy and a wallet that was always almost empty, a first-class seat was not what I was looking for.

The week before, I had broken up with a man I had dated for some time. I had hoped the relationship would end up at the altar, but it ended up nowhere. My reaction was to cut my losses and move on to new and better experiences. Easy to say, but I was really feeling sorry for myself. Now I had to be creative, and was trying to think up ways that would allow me to meet the type of man I would want to marry. I thought about this for a moment and decided to splurge on a first-class seat, just to see what all the fuss was about. Let's see if sitting in the high priced seats from LAX to SFO would prove to have added value.

I usually dressed in casual clothes – khakis and a blazer. I found that wearing long pants on an airplane was more comfortable because it was cold at 35,000 feet. Pants were easier to deal with. I was always pulling my skirt down, for fear of showing too much leg – I am five feet seven inches. But I was traveling first-class and on the lookout for romance, so I decided to wear a skirt and blazer. I thought that a little bit of my leg would not be too daring. Maybe it would work to my advantage!

It was boarding time. I took my seat and was handed a glass of champagne. I opened the first page of my novel, staring at it. The first-class cabin was full except for the seat next to me. My thoughts rumbled. *Will this first-class ticket be a total waste of money? What a bummer. I try to do something special and it just backfires.* I went back to reading.

All of sudden I heard shouting and doors slamming. I peeked from behind my book and saw a handsome man bounding through the slightly ajar door that the flight attendant was trying to close. My heart leaped. And yes, you guessed it – he was 2B, my seatmate! But just my luck, he was wearing a wedding ring. I thought. *Married. Huh. The ring rarely lies. Well, so much for my prince today. Where is the single guy I wanted to sit next to?*

What a shock. I didn't realize how agitated I had become with the anticipation of meeting my prince charming on this flight. However, my married seatmate seemed quite nice. He was well groomed, wearing a dark blue pinstripe suit and what appeared to be Italian loafers. His leather briefcase was so shiny that you could see yourself in it. He looked about 35. I made observations as nonchalantly as I knew how by stealing glances while pretending to read.

Suddenly, I started to sneeze. That was the icebreaker. He offered me a tissue and began to give me the third degree in a very nice way. Before long, I had spilled my abbreviated life history to him. He was interested in why an attractive young woman like me was not already married or involved with someone. After hearing me describe the type of man I wanted to meet, he asked for my telephone number in case he found someone who fit my requirements.

"Now, when was the last time you used that line?" I said while at the same time thinking to myself, *Sure, you are really going to find me my Prince Charming?* I took a leap of faith and gave this man my work phone number. I thought that this would be the end of our meeting. Finito! There was nothing more to discuss.

Well, I was proven wrong. Within a few weeks, I got a call from a man who had heard about me from my seatmate. The inquiring gentleman was his boss. He was planning a trip to Los Angeles and wanted to meet me.

We met for drinks at a chic Beverly Hills hotel. When our eyes first met, there was an instant spark. It's difficult to explain the emotions that well up inside you when this happens. Love at first sight, like a warm rush of sunshine.

It was hard to believe, but we were married within the year.

Susan's Lesson

Give yourself the freedom to move in different circles.
The more people you meet, the greater the likelihood of finding your soulmate.

A DISCUSSION OVER PRODUCE
PEPPER'S STORY

My divorce was final. This was a difficult period of my life. I married right after graduating from college. Now, after a 28 year marriage to the same man, and having three children with him, he left me for a younger woman. You hear stories like this, but you never think it could happen to you. Wrong — I was stunned. It took me about a year to emerge from my state of shock.

Four days after my divorce was final, still wearing tennis clothes from my early morning game, I stopped to buy produce in a local grocery store. For the first time in my life I was not responsible for anyone other than myself. My children were grown and starting lives on their own. I had to come to terms with this new life of mine. One item that I needed to deal with was what I wanted to eat. For years I was always shopping for foods that the majority of my family would eat. Now I only had to think of myself. *What do I want to eat today, and tomorrow?*

Somewhere between the lettuce and the tomatoes, I was mesmerized. I really couldn't focus on what I wanted to eat. While still in this trance-like stupor, a familiar voice called my name.

"Hi Pepper. What's happening? Is the divorce final?" It happened to be my friend Peggy. For years we shared a carpool taking our girls to ballet class.

I realized that I had not seen or spoken to Peggy for a very long time. My marital trauma made me a recluse. My divorce was my problem and I should not burden others with the gory details. In response I said, "Yes, the divorce was final four days ago. Now I need to start the next chapter of my life."

When she heard "yes" without skipping a beat, she added, "Can you attend a dinner party fundraiser tonight? I put a table together but one of the women just canceled. She's come down with the flu."

My first response was, "No. Get someone else. I haven't been in a social setting without my husband in 28 years. I have to move slowly in this direction." As soon as Peggy processed the "no" she was on my case.

"Pepper, just a minute. You have to move forward in your life. You aren't going to do that by staying at home. Listen, you owe me big time. I'm calling in all the chits from the extra ballet carpools I drove for you. You really owe this to me."

I tried to think of why I couldn't attend this event. No dress, nails not manicured, a headache, but I could not think up one good excuse. Reluctantly, I agreed to fill the empty seat at Peggy's table.

I was nervous as a girl going out on her very first date. *What do I wear? What do I say? Oh why did I say yes?*

The round table seated five men and five women. I was seated next to a charming bachelor, while four married couples rounded out the table. This arrangement felt so awkward. I certainly didn't want anyone to say, "Please pass the pepper." During the course of the evening, the bachelor, Michael, and I discovered we had many mutual interests including tennis and sailing. Our conversation was slow and easy. He made me laugh and smile through his good humor and thoughtful compliments on my little black cocktail dress. Later that night, Michael asked me to dance. He helped to pull my chair from the table and escorted me to the dance floor. There was only a moment of hesitation on my part when he took my hands in his and began a sensuous slow dance. This dance proved that I was still alive. For one year my heart felt dead, no emotion, a sick soul. In wonderment I questioned my feelings. *How did this almost total stranger have such power over me?* He made my heart sing. I sensed a glimmer of hope.

Michael was kind and a good listener. He was very careful with me, and didn't pry into my past. After the dinner we exchanged phone numbers. Michael had some business dealings that were going to occupy his time for several weeks but he said, "Pepper, I'd really like to see you again. Tonight felt special." And true to his word, he called.

Within one month of our meeting we both "fell in love." We married within a year and I'm so grateful that the produce department was on the top of my list.

♥

Pepper's Lesson

Being spontaneous may add spice to your life.

IT PAYS TO ANSWER THE PHONE
DAWN'S STORY

I always thought I'd just marry some guy I met in college. Instead, I found myself alone, approaching 27-years-old and wondering if there was a Mr. Right for me. I spent a lot of time reading magazine articles on how to meet men. I joined several organizations, and soon was volunteering to take reservations for a fundraiser expecting about nine hundred singles. Maybe it would gain me some extra visibility in the group.

Once the calls started coming in, I went nuts. Do you have any idea what my first two evenings were like? Calls, calls, and more calls, but all were short, impersonal, and informational. Then I decided not to answer my phone. Make believe like I'm not there! Thank goodness for answering machines. I stopped answering the phone and just sorted the personal calls towards the end of the evening. It worked like a charm. But one evening, on reflex, I answered the phone on the first ring. Some eerie process of destiny must have been at work.

He was the friendliest caller with the nicest voice. After a bit, he said, "I know we haven't met and this might be a little forward, but I'm having a party on Saturday night. There will be lots of people. If you and a girlfriend would like to come, I'd like to meet you." I was noncommittal. But when I hung up, I thought, *those magazine articles would say to go!*

Well, I went. The guy with the great voice didn't move me at all, but his best friend was so terrific that it was love at first sight. He had a great sense of humor, an infectious laugh, and a way of looking at me directly with his eyes that made my heart melt. I still can't believe that we were married in six weeks, but now it is over eight years of happiness later. Oh, and sometimes I still take the advice in those nutty magazine articles.

♥

Dawn's Lesson

Give a little and you may benefit exponentially.
Volunteer work may be an entrée to love.

IN THE LAND OF LA
LAUREN'S* STORY

If you know anything about living in Chicago, winter was usually cold, snowy and windy. By February, I was in a deep funk, and desperately needed a warm weather vacation. A girlfriend and I decided that Club Med, in Cancun, was just what we late twenty-somethings needed to warm our bones and perk up our faded winter spirits.

During our week long stay, we met a group of men from Los Angeles. One of these men was absolutely fabulous; tall, dark eyes, and handsome. He had a great body, was athletic, and had a wonderful sense of humor. Rich told me he only dated divorced women with kids when he was on vacation. This way he would not get too serious because he didn't want to get involved with a person with so much extra baggage. Since I didn't fit this mold – I was single with no kids, he was a little gun-shy about our instant attraction for each other.

Our vacation romance was delicious. We did all sorts of things together: swimming, sun bathing, snorkeling, and walking on the beach at sunset. My one-week in the sun with Rich certainly perked me up. I also met a good friend of his who was pretty cool too. When it was time to leave

Club Med, the three of us exchanged telephone numbers. My girlfriend and I went back to Illinois, and the guys went back to California.

Several months passed. I really had a crush on Rich, and couldn't get him out of my mind. He had made such an impact on me. During this time, I had no contact with him. Rich was true to his word about dating single women. Nevertheless, I had to do something about my infatuation, and decided to be the aggressor.

Calling his friend I said, "It's Lauren. Remember when we met in Cancun? You said anytime I wanted to come to Los Angeles to let you know. Is that offer still open to use your spare bedroom?"

He immediately replied, "Fine. When should I expect you?" Before I could change my mind, I packed my bags and was L.A. bound, the week before Easter.

After arriving in L.A., things were not quite as I remembered them. Rich, the guy I had a crush on at Club Med, didn't seem that interested in my surprise visit. I was a little hurt, but realized that Rich was not emotionally ready for a relationship. A vacation was one thing. Real life was something else. This explained his vow of only dating divorced women with kids because he would not get emotionally attached to them.

Even though my plan did not work, I wanted to make the most of my L.A. experience. Somehow I remembered that a girl who I casually knew from my hometown Cleveland also lived in L.A. When I phoned her, she was delighted that I took the effort to make contact, and invited me to go out to dinner with her and her boyfriend that night.

We met at a local restaurant and I was introduced to her boyfriend as "Lauren from Chicago." After a few minutes her boyfriend Rob said, "Lauren, I know we just met, but I have a friend who lives in Chicago and I think the two of you would really hit it off."

I thought to myself, *What had I done? I had gone cross-country to California only to be given the phone number of a man in my own city.*

After a fun evening together we promised to stay in touch.

When I returned to Chicago, I procrastinated about calling Rob's friend. It just felt awkward. About three months later, I was listening to a show on TV about women taking charge in the dating scene. Something sparked. I decided to take a gamble and called Andy, the Chicago friend.

"Hi. I'm Lauren. I met your friend Rob in L.A. and he gave me your number. Rob thought we'd have a lot in common and should meet."

I could tell that Rob was a good friend because Andy replied, "If Rob said we should meet, then I guess we should meet." Andy agreed to a time and place, at a local bar we both knew.

When I first saw him, it was love at first sight – my dream date. He was tall, thin, with a strong face, chiseled chin, and sparkling hazel eyes. I knew from the first moment that I met him I would be with him forever. He had a certain power over me. Andy felt the same way about me. He focused his attention on me when we talked and made me feel like I was on center stage. He was bowled over because he never realized that his friend Rob knew his taste in women so well.

Our first meeting was in August. By the following May, we were engaged. Eleven months later we were married. Even the best plans don't always work out the way you think they should, and in my case I am so glad they didn't.

Lauren's Lesson

If you procrastinate too long, an opportunity may cease to exist.

THE LAST NICKEL
LORRIE'S* STORY

It was World War II. In those days, it was common for people with extra rooms to rent them to servicemen on duty. This was both patriotic, and helped to make ends meet.

Soon after my mother posted a notice for our extra room (up on the third floor), Mrs. Lillian Greenberg came calling. A lovely lady from Chicago, Mrs. Greenberg wanted to be closer to her husband. He was in training for advanced radio communications at St. Louis University. She lived with us for several months until her husband was transferred overseas. She then moved back to Chicago.

A month later, my mother received a phone call. In those days, a phone call cost a nickel, a quart of milk cost a quarter, and one-dollar was a whole lot of money. My slight 37-year-old mother always answered the phone in an effervescent and friendly fashion, never knowing who was going to be on the other end. She always said to me, "Lorrie dear, your voice shows who you are."

On the other end was a man, quite anxious, asking to speak to Mrs.

*First name changed.

Greenberg. I remember my mother replying, "Mrs. Greenberg? She's a friend of yours? Well, I am so sorry to tell you, but she moved back to Chicago. You just missed her by a month. I haven't a clue how she can be reached. She didn't leave a forwarding number. I'm so sorry I can't help you. Good luck in finding her. Bye."

In those days, phone calls from strangers were rare. I asked mom what that conversation was about. All she said was someone was looking for Mrs. Greenberg. No more than five minutes passed and the phone rang again. This time, I happened to answer the phone. It was the same caller. The man on the other end of the line seemed so lonely. He was sure we must have some idea how to reach Mrs. Greenberg. He said his name was Lenny and he was in St. Louis to attend an Army Specialized Training Program. Mrs. Greenberg was his only contact in St. Louis.

His voice betrayed his sadness in not finding her. "Mrs. Greenberg is a family friend. My parents said I should call her and she would sort of be my family away from home. I'm from Chicago and was looking forward to seeing her."

When he said this, I took pity on him. Without even asking my mom for permission, I invited him over to the house for a meal. I didn't think there was any harm in doing this.

I invited my best girlfriend over for dinner the same night as Lenny so we could check him out together. If he turned out to be a dud, we could still save the evening. Girlfriends like to work in pairs and protect each other. When Lenny came to dinner the following night, both of us had fixed ourselves up as best we could. We both wanted to make a good impression. We donned our only pairs of silk stockings and rationed pink lipstick. The war had made these essentials very expensive and hard to find. At 17, neither of us had a steady beau.

Soon Lenny and my friend were going out regularly. After a few months, Lenny stopped over at my house. He confessed that his relationship with my best friend was not progressing. Before I knew it, I was spending more time with Lenny. We became an item, and he ultimately proposed. We waited until I was 19 to marry. We have now been husband and wife for over 50 years.

What is so interesting about my story is the chance of meeting Lenny. I later found out that the only reason Lenny called back a second time was to hear my mother's youthful and happy voice again. He was so lonely. He was taking a big gamble because he only had two nickels in his pocket. He used his last nickel on that second phone call. Lenny thoughtfully remembers, "That last nickel was the best investment of my life."

Lorrie's Lesson

Opening your heart and home may lead to great rewards.

PARLEZ VOUS FRANÇAIS?
BETSY'S STORY

Picture me happily married. It was not until my mid-thirties that I found the man of my dreams. We met at a party. I was not planning to go and you can guess the rest. Mark was tall, had dark wavy hair, and intense brown eyes that made your heart melt, and he also spoke fluent French. My French was of the high school variety, and very rusty. It was important for Mark to keep his French fluent because he traveled to France, at least four times a year on business. His specialty was selling antique violin bows. Not many people in the world claimed this profession.

I decided to surprise Mark for our second anniversary and brush up on my French vocabulary. He had invited me to accompany him on one of his business trips. My health club offered many other types of adult classes besides step aerobics and spinning. The monthly newsletter announced an eight-week conversational French class geared to the adult traveler. *Perfect for me, and I could combine exercise for the body with exercise for my mind!*

I enrolled in this class. There were 12 students; men and women, of all ages, some with no knowledge of French, and others like me who only had a minimal residual knowledge of the language. All of us had the common desire to learn enough French so that we would be understood while traveling in France, and not make *faux pas* like confusing *pomme* (apple) and *pomme de terre* (potato) in a restaurant. Who would want to be surprised with potatoes for dessert when you thought you were ordering an apple tart?

Our class met weekly on Wednesday nights. Everyone looked forward to this midweek escape. Even though I had been a member of my health club for several years, I did not know any of the other class participants. One gentleman stood out, Alan. He always dressed so nicely with coordinated sweaters and shirts and was so very dapper. He did not wear a wedding ring. It would never have crossed his mind to wear sweats or jeans, like the rest of the class. One evening, before class began, I tried to get to know him a little better with the ulterior motive of determining who of my single girlfriends I could fix up with him.

With my wedding ring in clear view I asked inquisitively, "Alan, you are so charming why aren't you married?"

Sweetly he replied, "I was married and have grown children. Been there, done that. I see no need to get married since I am not about to be a father again."

With that reply I became introspective. *None of the women I knew would want to date a man who had no interest in fathering a child. All of my friends, just like me, had a distinct nesting instinct.*

After this explanation, I left Alan alone and did not proceed with my usual haste in being a matchmaker. Alan was a nice guy but not the kind of dating material I needed for my single girlfriends.

Once the French class ended, I did not see Alan again for many months. My life was totally turned upside down. Nine months after the French class, my husband of almost three years was diagnosed with terminal cancer. I was a wreck. The only thing that kept me somewhat sane was exercise.

My friends were very concerned about my well-being. I was in a living hell. How do you deal with such torture, with no possibility of escape? One of my friends at the health club took me under her wing and decided I needed to incorporate weight training with my aerobic workouts. Now, I was exploring a part of the gym I had never ventured into before, the inner sanctum of the exercise elite, where free weights reigned supreme.

From out of nowhere came a familiar voice. "Betsy, long time no see. How are you? How is the new house? How's your husband?" asked Alan.

It was so comforting to hear his mellow voice. I explained my ill fortune and he expressed his concern with hope for a miracle. A week or so later he sent a note to my office with a clipping about an experimental cancer drug. Without thinking, I stuffed his note into my desk drawer and forgot about it.

Six weeks later I was cleaning my desk drawer at work. I was such a pack-rat. *Where did I get so much paper? Why did I save these scraps?* It had always been therapeutic for me to clean out a drawer and start over. As paper was fluttering to the trash bin, I noticed a card with several phone numbers. With abject curiosity I caught the card in mid-air. Oh yes, this was from Alan. He wrote all of his contact numbers. *I don't remember this.* And look, he wrote, "If you need anything at all please call me."

Upon reflex, I dialed the first telephone number on the card. I got an answering machine so I simply said, "Alan, I am sorry it has taken me so long to call you. These last six weeks have been a nightmare. You were so kind to give me all of your contact numbers. I hate to leave this message on the phone, but Mark has passed away. I know that you're a lawyer. Maybe you could explain a few legal issues to me."

Alan called me back and promptly asked, "How about lunch? I am free for the rest of my life!" the first joke anyone had made to me since my husband's death.

I replied, "That would be great. I've numerous legal questions and need to find an estate lawyer. Maybe you can help me find one."

Alan took pity on me, and helped me find legal representation since he did not specialize in probate work. He was such a Good Samaritan, a sensitive listener, and a totally understanding human being. Once we found an attorney to help with the estate work, I was able to relax a little.

One morning a few weeks later, Alan called me at work and inquired, "What are you doing for lunch today? Before I had a chance to reply he added, "If you're free, I'll pick you up at noon."

Not reading any hidden meaning into this offer, I responded, "Sure. That sounds like fun. I don't have to be back at the radio station until I go on the air for the 3:00 P.M. traffic and weather report."

Alan picked me up promptly at noon. I asked where we were going and all he said was, "Wait and see."

We drove across the Golden Gate Bridge in the direction of Sausalito, the beauty of my surroundings was intoxicating. For the past nine months I had been unaware of the outside world around me. I only remembered the feeling of walls caving in all around me with scarcely enough air to breathe.

"I thought we'd have a picnic," said Alan as he parked the car and hastened to open my door. "You should get more fresh air. It would do you a world of good. You look like you've have been locked in a closet." He opened the trunk of the car and pulled out, a blanket, some wine, sandwiches and some freshly cut flowers.

All of a sudden a flicker of romance danced in my head. I was quiet, while trying to understand the meaning of this outing. Alan spoke first. He told me about his divorce. He was emotionally wounded and it took him several years to heal. He continued with the following, " I know you're not in any shape for a relationship right now, but would you consider going up to wine country with me this weekend as friends? I took the liberty of getting a room with two beds."

We had a wonderful romantic encounter. But one issue remained between us. Any man I was going to involve myself with romantically, on a permanent basis, must be willing to father my child. Alan seemed adamant about not wanting to walk down that path again.

Even though we had a delightful, warm and sunny weekend together and Alan made me feel emotions I thought were dead I had to say, "I feel so wonderful in your presence but I must be true to my inner self. Any man I become romantically involved with must be willing to father a child with me." I wasn't even speaking marriage, but my biological clock was ticking and I wanted to be a mother. So much for a weekend fling. This proclamation scared Allen. We broke up before we were even an item. Worst of all, I lost a dear friend.

Something must have hit Alan hard because he took my ultimatum as a personal challenge. Two months later he called and asked to see me. It was then he confessed that he was desperately in love with me and it took him two months to realized what a joy it would be to have a second family.

My sad story ends happily. Alan proposed at a lookout over the Golden Gate Bridge and gave me his grandmother's diamond as an engagement ring. We had a beautiful wedding with friends and colleagues and now have a wonderful little girl who is our shared joy.

♥

Betsy's Lesson

When your life hits rock bottom and things look bleak, you only have one course of action: pick yourself up, dust yourself off, and start all over again. My story just proves that an innocent friendship can blossom into love.

UNITED WE FLY
CINDY'S* STORY

Trying to make out the driver's name, my eyes bore into the New York City Taxi Medallion mounted on the cabby's dashboard. I spelled it out. "M-B-Z-G-V-R-S-G-B-T." *How could that be?* Somehow, I had managed to find myself in the hands of a guy who not only didn't have any vowels in his name, he didn't know how to find the Newark Airport. I slid back into the seat and tried to find a sign pointing us in the direction of the Holland Tunnel. "Hey, we're going north...we want to go west towards the Hudson," I shouted over the din of the pulsing salsa that screamed back at me from the cab's rear speakers. I simply wasn't going to make my plane unless a global positioning device miraculously appeared in the 2 x 3 ft. black portfolio case I used to transport my advertising layouts.

It was turning out to be that kind of evening. I should have known better than to grab a quick dinner with my brother Mark, who suffers from terminal lack of watch. His sense of time defied anything in this dimension. The small Upper East Side café, where he promised to meet me promptly at 3:00 P.M., was charming and great for people-watching the first ten minutes of the wait. As the clock ticked closer to 4:00 P.M. and his grinning bearded face just then peeked around the corner, I knew I was on thin ice.

I thought I could manage my anger and not yell at him for being late again. We'd have a diet coke and a fast review of his current girlfriend and job woes. Then I'd grab a cab going across 69th Street and speed my way through town to the Newark Airport, arriving in time to check my bulging garment bag, portfolio case and tote. I'd then walk leisurely to the gate with boarding pass in hand.

Mark's endless recounting of how Elise had done him wrong, and how his boss betrayed him, combined cruelly to tax my tightly-scheduled sojourn. When I finally stepped out onto the street and hailed a cab, I was in big trouble. I needed a "follow that car and step on it kind of ride." This little joy ride with Mr. No-Vowels didn't resemble that in the least. Finally, I spotted a sign for the Holland Tunnel. I held on tightly to my armrest as the cabby made a sweeping right turn and we were headed, at last, in the direction of the Newark airport.

When we finally drove up the ramp leading to United's departure terminal, it was one minute before six. My plane was the last flight of the evening, due to depart for San Francisco at 5:50 P.M. I didn't know whether to have the cab wait and take me to the nearest hotel or just go through the ridiculous exercise of pretending the plane was still there, just waiting for me to stroll up leisurely to check in. After a moment's deliberation, I figured my driver couldn't find his way back to Manhattan let alone a Holiday Inn. With way too exuberant a tip for the quality of the journey, I hopped out and made my way in the direction of the security area.

Naturally, I managed to get behind a man who set off the metal detector each time he tried to pass through. With each shriek of the device, he stepped back and pawed through pockets, as my blood pressure started to soar. I had to make my flight. I had an important meeting early the next morning and this man's Swiss Army knife, hidden in the bowels of his jacket, stood between me, and my flight home. I hoisted my bags up onto the conveyor and flew through the airport security gate with a rush of exhilaration. They weren't going to delay me a second longer!

Forget the reality of the clock that was inching its way to five minutes past six. I huffed and puffed with the weight of my luggage and began a slow jog down the endless hallway to the gate. Sweat broke out on my forehead as I began to see the circle of departure gates that lay ahead of me. I could not even stop to check the monitors. I was blindly focused on catching a plane that was scheduled to leave ten minutes earlier.

I was clearly in denial until a voice marred my swirl of single-minded fantasies. "Are you trying to catch the plane to San Francisco?" the voice inquired. "If you are, it's running late." Those words hit me like a brick. My adrenaline slid down faster than my garment bag off my shoulder. The voice chattered on. "Here, leave your stuff with me. I'll watch your carryons while you check in." I let my heavy tote bag slide off my shoulder and watched as my fingers, frozen around the handle of my portfolio case, slowly uncurled.

All I could think of was getting my miracle, my boarding pass. I made my way to check-in, showed my ID, and performed the other rituals. "No, no one else has touched my bags since I packed them. No, I haven't left them out of my control." I intoned in my bald-faced lie. I had just handed over my bags to a faceless stranger. *Out of my control?* He could be a foreign agent, stuffing my innocent suitcases with cocaine at this very moment. I smiled weakly up at the agent as she handed me my boarding pass.

Relieved, my eyes started to scan the crowd to find out with whom I had entrusted my stuff. Thirty feet away stood my portfolio case, garment bag and tote at the feet of a tallish, brown-haired man. Obviously he was a drug lord, preying on innocent women running late for flights, catching them in a weak moment. How could I let myself be taken in? I was a seasoned traveler. I never let a stranger approach me. Nonetheless, I needed to take control of my bags. It was a Lockerbie disaster waiting to happen!

I strutted over and grabbed my bags without making eye contact. "Hey!" he said, "Just leave them here. The plane doesn't start boarding for another ten minutes or so."

I stared at him with a look usually reserved only for reviled ex-boyfriends. He pressed on. "What seat do you have?" as he pointed towards the boarding pass tightly clutched in my fist. I slowly released my death grip and read tonelessly, "17H." He smiled and said, "You're kidding! I am in 17G." Uh, oh…I was going to be sitting next to him, my own little terrorist for six hours, just waiting for the entire plane to erupt into flames. Then he said, "Wanna switch? I am traveling with my work buddy and he is in 42C and we really want to sit together."

Now, I became incensed. I pulled myself up to my full height of five feet one inch and said, "No you can't have my window seat!" This man was utterly outrageous. One moment he's taking control of my bags, next my precious window seat.

I breathed a sigh of relief when they announced early boarding privileges for Frequent Fliers. I yanked my bags onto my shoulders and strode for the door of the jetway. "Hey, get us some extra pillows!" he yelled. I wanted to raise my finger in the ultimate salute as I thought, *get your own damn pillows*, but I couldn't raise my arm with all the weight I was carrying.

I boarded the plane quickly. Tucking my luggage in the overhead compartment and grabbing a blanket and pillow for myself, I settled into my home for the next six hours. I put my nose into my Robert Ludlum novel and turned my body to face the window. Finally, the would-be drug-dealer and international assassin sat down next to me. He had managed to find his own pillow and neatly stuck it in the small of his back. He stared at my left shoulder and coughed.

"Are you from San Francisco or Jersey?" he asked. I couldn't believe he had the nerve to try to talk to me. Didn't he know I never talked to anyone on planes? My mother would always claim I wouldn't even talk to her on a flight when we were traveling together. Usually I try to read a book. But mostly I prefer to use the time to catch up on sleep. I didn't want to get involved in any conversations with sweet little grandmas with 16 grandchildren flying their first flight from Topeka or some single guy who wanted my phone number. I wanted to be alone in flight. It was my own personal mantra. It was my space just for me, away from nagging clients, tight deadlines and whining bosses. But now this stranger was trying to invade not only my luggage but also my space.

I pushed my face deeper into my book. He continued on, undaunted, settling in by bringing down his tray table and setting his glasses on it. "I take this flight every week to San Francisco and it's never on time." I continued to ignore him. "This is the first time my associate is going to San Francisco. He's taking over for me on this account. It would have been good if we had the time to chat together on the flight about what he will be doing, but I can understand you not wanting to give up your window seat. If you get sleepy or anything, you can feel free to lean on my shoulder. I won't mind."

The man had lost his mind. His was the worst pickup line I ever heard. I glanced over at him just to see if he was for real. At just that moment, the flight attendant began her pre-flight announcements. "Put all tray tables up and bring your seat to the upright and locked position". He continued to chat. "I've been working at C&H Sugar."

The flight attendant slid past and requested again that he put up his tray table. He was intent on his conversation and on me. Out of my left eye, as if in slow motion, I saw him lifting the tray table up. His eyes never left me as he snugly tucked the tray table into its locked position. With that last bit of oomph, the sound of broken glass ground into the air as his eyeglasses smashed to smithereens. I couldn't help but laugh. "I guess you'll be getting contacts tomorrow," I quipped. For the first time I looked into his golden brown eyes. I thought to myself that those eyes should never be hidden behind glasses anyway. I snuck my book into the pocket in front of me. It kept the in-flight magazine company for the next six hours, while I got to know Sam and his very soft shoulder. It made a perfect pillow when my eyes closed and I finally drifted off into a pleasant sleep.

Two years later, almost to the day, Sam and I were married. Guests who flew in from out of town to enjoy the proceedings said how miraculous it was for two people living on opposite sides of the country to find each other. I said I didn't find him; United Airlines assigned him to me.

♥

Cindy's Lesson

First impressions can be misleading. Listen, and love may be revealed.

A SUBWAY MEETING
SHIRLEY'S STORY

Julia Richmond, the all girls high school in New York City, was home to six thousand students. As much as I loved my school, at the age of seventeen, I really liked attending dances sponsored by other groups because it put me in contact with boys! A group of girls would usually go to these events together, rather than be paired on a date.

Dancing had always been a favorite activity. I was very comfortable on a dance floor. One day, at a dance my youth group sponsored, a new boy appeared. He was actually a little older, and had been invited to attend the dance by Charlotte, one of the other girls in the club. This was his first encounter with the youth group. I thought he was nice. Since I was a good friend of Charlotte's and a better dancer than most of the other girls, he asked me to dance. He danced well, but his personality seemed a little quiet for me. Maybe it was because he was new to the scene. Surprisingly, after the dance ended, Bob asked me for my telephone number.

Within a week, Bob was calling me regularly. We went out a couple of times on casual dates. I thought he was nice looking and kind, but he didn't make my heart go "pitter patter." The end of school was near and my high school graduation was almost a reality. I was not mentally interested in continuing any of my high school romances. My next focus was on college. Fortunately I was accepted at New York University, my first choice, where the ratio of college men to women was 5 to 1. After an all girls high school, college would be like heaven.

Bob continued to call. In his typical no-nonsense fashion he would say, "Hi Shirley. How about a movie? You pick the night. Any night this week is good with me."

Enthralled with my new college world, I had no time for him on my social calendar. I did not want to be rude to him. Bob was persistent in his efforts to date me, but I did not encourage his interest. There were no fireworks. Bob was a very nice man but I really wanted to explore all my new dating options. After a while, Bob stopped calling. I really didn't think twice about it because I was having such fun dating other college men.

Four years went by. One night I was getting off the C line subway going home to the Bronx. It was at the height of the rush hour. I had an early date that evening. After pushing my way through the throngs of people at the turnstile, I finally made it to the stairs going up to street level.

Over the whir of the subterranean noises associated with a train about to depart from the platform someone was shouting, "Hey Shirley. Remember me? Are you married? Can I call you? What's the number?"

When I heard the name "Shirley" I turned around and spotted a guy on the platform below who was madly waving his arms. It was my attention he was trying to catch. It was Bob from my distant past about to enter the train I had just departed. I yelled back, "Not married. Same number."

Bob later told me that those were magic words. He had memorized my telephone number years before and had never gotten it out of his mind – Jerome 89032 was permanently embedded in his brain. He had often thought about calling me, but was too gun-shy because I had not encouraged his advances years ago. Now, he got the chance he was waiting for.

About a week later he called. We made a date to go out to dinner the next evening. My memory of him before that dinner was vague. Four years in the life of a 21-year-old was an eternity. Bob's big news was that he was being shipped off to boot camp the next day and would have a three-month stint before his next assignment related to World War II.

For the first time, I saw Bob as a warm, engaging, handsome young man, who also had a deep sense of commitment and honor in defending the freedoms of the United States. Something happened on this dinner date that sealed my fate. Through this second chance, we both knew that we were meant for each other. There was an unspoken bond between us – call it destiny.

Our conversation just flowed with endless laughter and ease. We discovered our mutual love of music and he reminded me of being a great dance partner years earlier. Bob confessed that he had a fabulous singing voice and started to mimic other famous singers of the day. He had me mesmerized. The evening went so well, we made arrangements for me to visit him at boot camp.

Three months later we were married. That was over 50 years ago.

Shirley's Lesson

You never know when the past may become a part of your future.

THE ELEVATOR UPS AND DOWNS
GINNY'S STORY

My parents divorced when I was a teenager. After this traumatic experience, any meeting with my father and stepmother was trying. My stepmother had totally alienated my dad from me, so what was the point? I was periodically required to have lunch with my father, a meeting far better than having lunch with both. Even so, it was so difficult for me to be alone with him. I found that if I brought along one of my girlfriends for moral support, my father would be on better behavior and the luncheon meeting would be less of an inquisition and more like an interview.

On this particular day for our father-daughter lunch (my 25th birthday to be exact), I invited a girlfriend from college to accompany me. We met at the Bankers Club on the top floor of the Bank of America Building in San Francisco. It is typical of a men's business club with dark paneled walls, discreetly spaced tables, and whispering guests. You could hear the clicking of glasses and faintly smell cigar smoke in the air. After a tedious lunch, my father informed me that I was expected to have dinner with him and my stepmother that same night. Two meals with him in the same day was just too much to ask. These family duties were simply unbearable to me. If you witnessed their behavior toward me you'd understand. I just couldn't do these meals alone. This announcement was the signal that our lunch was over. My girlfriend and I excused ourselves and made a beeline to the elevator.

As we entered the elevator to transport us from this private San Francisco enclave back to the real world, I turned to my girlfriend. Before I could say anything she announced, "I know what you are thinking and the answer is no." She punctuated this emphatically by hitting the elevator button to the ground floor. I only had a few minutes with her held captive in the elevator (51 floors) until we hit ground level, hopefully enough time for me to change her mind about dinner.

My girlfriend could really stir up attention. I must say both of us were knockouts in the figure and looks department especially when we were dressed in our little suits and high heels. At lunch we observed sly looks of envy toward my father sitting across the table from us twenty-something girls.

Somewhere between the 51st floor and the 30th, a handsome young man entered our elevator. He was dressed in a dark business suit, had sandy brown hair, and gentle eyes. He had the physical features that could really turn heads. My first impression was he could easily be a model. I am sure he heard every word of our female banter while feigning disinterest. With only 30 more floors I had to act fast. Spontaneity had always been one of my traits. Without skipping a beat, knowing I had nothing to lose, I turned to this young man, whom I had never seen before. We locked eyes and I asked, "How about you? Would you like to go to dinner with me tonight?"

There was a moment of silence that seemed to last an eternity. *Did I need to repeat the invitation? Did he speak and understand English? Was he so shocked at the offhanded invitation that he was speechless?* I felt as if I was walking on a tightrope and in one breath would either make it to the end of the line or fall into oblivion. *Why did I get myself into such sticky situations?* To my astonishment he said, "Yes!"

And you can guess the rest of the story. My elevator pickup became my husband.

♥

Ginny's Lesson

Doing something spontaneous may have surprising consequences.

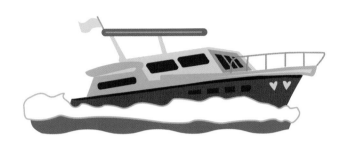

CONVENTIONS *ARE* NOT ALL BUSINESS
SANDRA'S STORY

I'm from a small town in Virginia. It's the kind of place where everyone knew everything about everybody. My Southern background was quite obvious because of my distinctive drawl!

Fourteen years ago, I was in the prime of my life with a teenage son and an ex-husband who continued to be part of our lives. I had a great job as a principal of an elementary school.

Once in a while, I had to attend a convention or meeting away from home but rarely did it require travel overnight. So, you can understand my total shock and amazement when I received a phone call from the district superintendent one week before the National Principal's Convention. He was asking me if I could attend in place of another woman, who'd just phoned with a medical emergency.

Did it take me long to answer this request? "Good golly, San Francisco? My bags are packed!" It had been years since I'd had the opportunity to feel the fog, see the wonderful Golden Gate Bridge, and taste the sophistication and excitement of one of the most beautiful cities on earth. What a surprise phone call! But was there an ulterior motive? *What on earth made the superintendent choose me?*

The next few days were a whirlwind. I had to make sure many duties were assigned to other people so that my responsibilities would be shared in my absence. For this occasion, I also had to get a haircut and a manicure – pure indulgence, and do a little shopping to spruce up my everyday look. San Francisco demanded more than my basic knit pants and coordinated tunic top.

On the first day, the convention ended about 4:00 P.M. The agenda was very interesting; the outside scenery spectacular. The St. Francis Hotel was known for its glass elevators. Just riding this steel-and-glass box to my room allowed me to view the world beyond. From my perch inside the elevator, it was possible to scan the horizon from the Golden Gate Bridge to Alcatraz and all the way to the Bay Bridge. There was a golden aura in the sky caused by the refraction of sunlight through a very faint mist. At 5:00 P.M. it would still be light outside for a few more hours because of daylight savings time. Now would be the perfect time to explore San Francisco.

Another female principal joined me on a trip to Fisherman's Wharf. The cable car stop was conveniently located in front of the hotel. What a quaint and lovely way to take public transportation! Feet dangling, hair flying, to-die-for-views – all for the same price as an ordinary bus! It was now about 6:00 P.M. but it was 9:00 P.M. on our body clock. All of a sudden, we looked at each other and cried in unison, "Food!" We found a restaurant that was open, not yet too busy, and did not require a reservation. Soon we were seated in the dining room next to the only other occupied table.

At first, I was only interested in the breathtaking view from our seats. Docks filled with small fishing boats flying colorful sails made a very artistic picture. I thought. *Wouldn't it be spectacular to cruise the Bay in one of those boats?*

The other table included two couples and a single man. The two women (we later learned) had been secretaries to the single man. This was the third date the couples had made to go sailing on the Bay with the former boss. The other two dates had been canceled because of an illness and a business trip.

And then it happened. The single man made eye contact with me. At that moment, I whispered to my companion, "Just you wait. As God is my witness, we're going to have a visitor at our table before the night is through." And, mark my word he soon came over to talk to me.

He said that he was enchanted with my Southern drawl. I admit it was hard to hide that drawl from anyone. I can't even hide my voice. You can imagine that a principal's voice isn't soft and sweet. I was used to being an authority figure at my school.

Soon, the three of us were engrossed in a lively conversation. Our gentleman visitor asked if we had plans for the evening. Would we like to join him and his friends on his boat for a sunset Bay cruise? *God has answered my prayers! How do you say "No" to that kind of invitation?* So I said to him, "That sounds like a line right out of the movies. And, we're going to fall for it!"

Bob held my chair as I moved from the table and then quickly reached for my forearm as if to guide me to the next chapter in my life.

To this very day, I am so grateful for the circumstances that brought us together. Had it not been for the other principal's cancellation, I would not have had the chance to leave my heart in San Francisco! Had Bob's date with his office staff not been postponed, we might not have met. So many things needed to be just right, but it happened!

I have now been cruising with him since 1990!

Sandra's Lesson

When travel opportunities for work arise, embrace them.
Dare to dream, and your dreams may come true.

WALKING ON THE FRENCH RIVIERA
DENISE'S STORY

I was a flight attendant flying home to San Diego after a transatlantic run from L.A. to Milan. I took a short layover on the French Riviera because a few days of R&R were needed. Being a flight attendant was not as glamorous as one might think. You were never alone. People always asked you for something. Privacy was difficult to find. But it also had an advantage – free travel to interesting places.

Early in the afternoon, I was walking down the main street by the outdoor cafés in the city of Cannes with another female flight attendant. It was a beautiful fall day. The air was balmy and the Mediterranean a sparkling azure blue. I was wearing white formfitting cropped pants, a pink halter-top and a rather large straw hat. My girlfriend and I cut a striking pair. We had a bounce and *joie de vivre* to our steps. Of course we both wore the obligatory dark sunglasses.

All of a sudden, we heard someone yell in our direction. We couldn't tell where this voice was coming from. With a quick survey of the scene, we continued to saunter down the street. I surmised, "I guess that was meant for someone else."

We were used to catcalls, whistles and the like. We really didn't do anything to provoke these occurrences. I guess it was our blond hair and nice figures. Now, all of a sudden, there was a man at my side. Speaking English, he pleaded with us to stop and have a drink with him and his friend. Exasperated, we replied, "No, thank you."

He was so excited to hear that my friend and I spoke English that he blocked our path and continued to persuade us to join them. *At least we will be able to hold a conversation with these men; they will not be speaking French.* Instead we replied, "What the heck," and agreed to join them for a *café au lait.*

He led us over to the table where his friend was reading an American newspaper. My first question was, "Are you from the States?"

The friend answered, "Bingo, right on the mark. How'd you ever know that?" It turned out that they were both from California, just like me. They were in France on business and worked in the garment industry.

My friend and I agreed to meet them for dinner. We had a very nice evening but nothing romantic. I was rather nonchalant about the entire experience. I was still sort of in love with a charming man who lived in Milan. Deep within myself, I agonized over my relationship with this Italian that had stalled like a Ferrari out of gas. Men…

I didn't feel any chemistry with my pursuer because he was too sarcastic. His friend was more my type. He had a good sense of humor, a fun-loving attitude and he didn't take himself too seriously. Unfortunately, he didn't seem interested in me.

After dinner, I gave my San Diego telephone number to these two men because we were all leaving the Riviera the next day. They were going to contact me for a weekend of modeling jeans at a garment convention in San Diego. This sounded like fun to me and I could pick up a few extra dollars. I flew home, arranged to get that specific weekend off work and waited for their phone call.

Days turned into weeks, and weeks turned into months. No telephone call. I was quite miffed. These men were adamant about calling to set up the jeans assignment. It had been almost a year since our meeting. Then one day, my Italian class had a dinner at a local Tuscan-style restaurant. And there he was, one of the Riviera men. I remembered him instantly because he had a striking full head of curly jet-black hair. I think he saw me at the same moment I saw him. It was the man who'd been reading the paper, the guy that I thought was *more my type*. He came right over to where I was sitting and greeted me like a long lost friend. I was rather tentative, because I was still wondering why they never called. As it turned out the other man forgot to give Larry, who was in charge of the models, my contact information.

He started to reminisce about our last meeting, recounting even the most minuscule details about our brief encounter. My thoughts were a mixture of confusion and surprise, *I must have really made an impact!* I asked about his friend. He'd since married a woman he had been dating on and off for the past five years.

Larry and I slowly developed into a couple. He was kind, courteous and had a deep Santa Claus-style laugh. I could see in his eyes that he really cared for me, and over time, my eyes twinkled back.

We dated for two years, and then married. What a crazy chance of fate that I stopped to talk to total strangers six thousand miles from home!

Denise's Lesson

It always pays to be nice.

PLEASE LIGHT MY FIRE
GEORGIA'S STORY

My younger sister was totally different from me. Anne was beautiful with golden ringlets and a dainty manner. She was all girl, preferring to wear dresses and to play with dolls. I was the tomboy type. My short bobbed brown hair and lanky legs were quite a contrast from my sister. Nothing made me happier than wearing jeans and climbing trees.

My family was devoutly Catholic. For years my parents tried to have more children than just the two of us, but the stork never visited again. My mom and dad felt that the greatest gift to a parent would be a child who would serve God. They hoped to have a son who would become a priest.

At the age of ten, my parents sent me to live in a convent. I often wondered how my parents decided which child to send to God. Maybe it was because I was not as beautiful or dainty as my sister, and they thought I would have a harder time finding a man to marry.

For 20 years I stayed in the convent. But at the age of 30 I developed misgivings about my chaste existence, and yearned for a change.

It was decided that I could leave the convent since it was not solely my decision to become a nun in the first place. To make the transition to life outside the church easier for me, the sisters rummaged through some Salvation Army boxes for donated street clothes, basic household items, and also found an old bicycle that could be used for transportation. They even gave me a small amount of money so I could rent an apartment. I would have to find a job, but that would come later.

Being on my own was a dream come true, but it also had many challenges.

I found an apartment on a quiet tree-lined street. It was on the second floor. I never experienced that kind of privacy. The apartment was small but adequate…one bedroom, tiny bath, living room/dining room combination and a little kitchen. Plenty of space for me.

The first day I took possession of my apartment was a grand event. When I rang the bell of the building manager's apartment I tingled with excitement and said, "Hi. I am Georgia, I'm here to pick up the keys for apartment 18."

"Welcome dear," was the reply from the building manager who looked to be well into her 80s. She continued, "Here are two sets of keys. Everything checked out in fine working order when I did my inspection yesterday. I hope you'll be very happy here. If you need anything just ring my bell."

I flew up the stairs. This was the moment I had been waiting for and thought, *finally, my very own place and a return to secular life.* By no means was I upset with the convent. It was just that I wanted to see for myself, if a nun's life was my true destiny.

I had one small bag with me since I rode over on my bike. The rest of my things would be delivered by the parish van later in the day. I had brought a sandwich and an apple and my favorite tea. I was ready to eat lunch.

I was not very domestic. The sisters had given me a few cooking lessons so I could boil water, make scrambled eggs and mix my favorite tuna salad. They said that cooking was as simple as reading a book. I would learn.

The stove did not work. I remembered that the building manager said everything was in working order. *What was the problem?* Whenever I turned a knob to "on" I got a heavy whiff of gas. This concerned me. *Oh where was that darn pilot light?* Death by a kitchen stove was not the way I wanted to end my life.

The first person I tried was the building manager. *No answer, just when I really needed her.*

Next, I rang my neighbor's bell. A nice looking man who looked to be between 30 and 40 answered the door.

"Hi. I'm Georgia your new neighbor. Sorry to bother you, but do you think you could help me light the pilot light on my stove?"

"Sure," he said while giving me that head-to-toe once-over look. He then chuckled under his breath and commented, "that's the best pickup line I've ever heard."

He was very easy to talk to, and for some reason he opened up to me instantly saying, "I feel so peaceful in your presence, so serene." It turned out he had just gone through a messy divorce. He was the first man I met after leaving the convent.

He certainly did light my fire. I was the breath of fresh air he needed, and he was my answer to ending my chaste existence. He became my rock and salvation. We have now been married for over 20 years!

♥

Georgia's Lesson

Step into your dreams. Be yourself,
not the person you imagine others want you to be.

IT PAYS TO PRAY
PEARL'S STORY

I was 26 and traveling to California for the first time. Being from Chicago, my impressions of California included: blue sky, sunshine, and a landscape dotted with palm trees. My mother and I arranged to take this ten-day trip together. We thought it would be a good bonding experience, since my high school teaching schedule kept me quite busy. Upon arriving in Los Angeles, we were going to stay with several different sets of relatives we had not seen in years. My mom had a saying "after three days fish smell." It meant unpacking and repacking several times, but it was going to be a wonderful family reunion.

Our trip was crammed with excitement and fun. We saw family, friends, and the tourist sights of L.A. including: Rodeo Drive with all its classy designer shops, Grauman's Chinese Theatre, and the Santa Monica area near the Pacific Ocean. We were busy morning 'till night. On the last Friday night of our trip we were invited to go to a cocktail party at a friend's home. Since the party didn't start until eight o'clock, we decided at the last minute that we also had time to go to an early religious service with cousin Bertha.

I always loved the part of the service where there was a silent prayer, where you could think about the special needs of your family and your life. This was when you sit down with God in your private world. Since I was not married, and had no steady boyfriend, my silent prayer always included a request to God to find me a Mr. Right.

After the services, the congregation sponsored a social hour with coffee, punch, and cookies. Mom and I looked at our watches to gauge how much time we had before our next event of the evening and said in unison, "Fifteen minutes is all we have. Let's make the most of it!" We started to mingle with some of the other people who had attended the service.

My cousin spied another cousin of hers, at the far end of the room and motioned for her to come over to meet us. This cousin was related to Bertha through her father rather than through her mother, like us. With Bertha's other cousin Dorothy, was Roy her brother, who was on a two-week leave from the Air Force. They had decided at the last minute to go to services too.

Bertha introduced mom and me and said, "Dorothy, these are cousins Ida and her daughter Pearl from my mom's side of the family. I think I told you I was going to have house guests from Chicago."

"Delighted to meet both of you," I replied. I felt my face get hot with a blush, as I looked straight in to Roy's chocolate drop eyes.

He was tall, about five feet ten inches, with dark hair, and looked very important wearing his dress Air Force uniform with rows of medals and buttons on his breast-pocket that signified his accomplishments. He fit my mental image of a prince charming. I started a modest conversation by asking, "Where are you from?"

Roy answered, "I am from a small town in Ohio. At the last minute I decided to take my two weeks of military leave, and get out of the cold February winter to see my sister Dorothy who recently married and moved to Los Angeles. I've never been to California before."

Roy and I only had 15 minutes, but during this time I was spellbound by his quiet charm. I had never felt anything like it before. I had dated plenty of men but no one had ever affected me this way.

Roy must have been smitten with me too, because he immediately asked, "I know we have only just met, but I'd really like to keep in touch. May I call you sometime?" Roy explained that his leave was over and that he was flying back to Ohio the next day.

We returned to our hometowns and kept in touch through frequent letters and phone calls. After a few months we started to visit each other on the weekends. Our mutual fondness grew into love. We married two years after we first met. It was so totally by chance that we happened to be at the same place at the same time, two thousand plus miles away from our homes. God really listened to my silent prayer that night!

Pearl's Lesson

If you believe in yourself, opportunities may come your way.

PRINCE CHARMING RESCUES CINDERELLA
JAYNE'S STORY

At 32, I was recently divorced and left with a young son. Just like all ten-year-old boys, he was constantly getting dirty. Thus, my laundry hamper was always full.

We had just moved to an apartment building in a very nice area of San Francisco – Pacific Heights. A key feature of this building was the on-site laundry facility located on the parking level.

During the day, I held a high-powered job at Macy's as vice-president of merchandising. My usual work outfit was a fashion-packed power suit, heels, and not a hair out of place. As a single mother, my schedule was non-stop from morning until night. Work, child issues, and housekeeping tasks kept me busy. I rarely went out on dates. Men were not a prime interest after my ill-fated first marriage. Usually, I went home immediately after work and put on blue jeans or sweats. I pulled my long blond hair in a ponytail and scrubbed off all my makeup. Next, I would make dinner, do homework with my son or tackle the laundry.

One night when I was busy sorting clothes, a man I had never seen before walked into the laundry room. He was actually looking for another entrance but went into the laundry room by mistake.

My heart skipped a beat. He was dressed from head to toe in Armani and cut a most striking figure. I was speechless. He literally took my breath away. I was extremely embarrassed with my no-frills appearance and wanted to hide. My visitor, oblivious to my predicament, then stated, "Hi there, I'm Marc. I'm new to this building and recently divorced with two young children. Do you know any babysitters?"

It took me a moment to gain my composure. I proceeded to reply, not sure if words would form from my mouth since I was still in shock from gazing upon this Prince Charming. "Sure, I know a few babysitters. I have a young son, and went through a divorce not long ago too. I'll be glad to get you some names and phone numbers."

That night I could not stop thinking about this man. *Was it a dream? Was he for real? Did he really live in my building?* Later that night, I slipped out of my apartment and put a note with the babysitter information under his door. I also included my phone number. The next day, Marc called to thank me for my help and asked if my son and I would like to join him and his two kids for a casual outing that weekend.

Saturday finally came with much anticipation. Three screaming kids and two adults piled into his 380 Mercedes sports car. Our first date was anything but romantic, but I was impressed with his suave and debonair looks, genuine kindness and his love for his children.

We became a laundry room romance. Prince Charming rescued Cinderella. We were married in September the following year. And as he still says to all of his friends, "I've never seen Jayne in the laundry room since."

Jayne's Lesson

Love can lurk in the most surprising places.

CRUISING THE PARK
JOAN'S STORY

Let me set the stage for my story: senior in college at Washington University in St. Louis, graduation was just two months away and all my required classes were finished. I had one final paper to write, and two final exams that I dreaded. St. Louis was not known for its weather. It was either cold or swelteringly hot, with nothing in between. It seemed that winter turned into summer almost immediately.

One beautiful spring day I decided it was too nice to be cooped up in classes. This was just the kind of opportunity I needed to try out my new convertible. Very snazzy: an advance graduation gift from my parents, coupled with six years of savings from summer jobs. Classes and homework would have to be put on hold until I had my ride in the park. It was a huge decision for me to cut classes, but the urge to drive my new convertible was so compelling I just gave in and risked any consequences.

Cruising the park near my college campus, I spotted the usual cyclists and walkers. Then I spotted something curious: a nice looking man waxing his car.

Just as I was cruising past him he yelled in my direction, "Nice set of wheels." I stopped to take a closer look at the person making the compliment. Normally, I wouldn't react to a comment made in this manner.

"Is this business or pleasure?" I asked, really meaning, *Do you wash cars for others or just your own?*

He replied, "It's so nice outside I decided to take the day off from work. I'm in sales and have flexibility with my schedule. My car was in desperate need of a spring-cleaning and I had to get rid of all those salt stains from winter. There is a lot more space to work on a car in the park than in the driveway of my apartment building." He went back to waxing his car.

He then asked, "So what brings you to Forest Park today?"

"I had to try out my new graduation present and make sure the convertible top worked properly," I said. He didn't need to know that I was cutting classes to facilitate my joy ride.

Something about him moved me more than words. He had taken off his shirt and I could already see the pale pink effect of the strong afternoon sun on his torso. I could see this guy was in darn good condition by the shape of his pecs and biceps. His face had a beautiful chiseled quality to it and his eyes just pierced through my soul.

Something must have moved him about me too, because he asked, "Would you like to go to the movies sometime?"

Without hesitation we exchanged names. He called me the next day and we had our first official date using his newly waxed car. Cutting classes that day did not cut anything from my life. Instead it shaped my entire future. We only dated for a few months, and married shortly after graduation. "Timing is everything. I'm now a firm believer in that!"

♥

Joan's Lesson

By changing your schedule and approach to life, a hidden gem may surface.

THE FIX UP THAT NEVER HAPPENED
SYLVIA'S STORY

One day in May a guy named Bruce called one of his best friends in San Francisco. Bruce was on his way to Asia for his Army posting and learned that he would have a two-day layover in the City by the Bay. Like many single men, Bruce wanted to make the most of his time before going overseas so he requested that his friend Rich fix him up with a great woman. Rich was delighted to help Bruce. All was arranged, and Bruce had a date for the Saturday he would be in town.

A few days before Bruce was to arrive in San Francisco he called Rich, "Sorry to inform you but my travel plans have been changed. My flight has now been routed through Los Angeles rather than SF. You are just going to have to tell my date it wasn't meant to be."

Rich understood that schedules changed.

Now my story begins. Fast-forward about three years. I'm Sylvia. a petite blond from San Francisco visiting the Big Apple with my girlfriends. We sat at the bar in a club on First Avenue, on the Upper East Side. It was a dimly lit room with piano music wafting in the background. I had one physical feature that often turned heads — I was very well endowed (you get the drift). My chest often made men's heads turn and tonight was no different. I was getting lots of sly glances from the male customers.

As I observed my surroundings I spied a single man at the far end of the bar. While giving him an inviting glance, I turned to my girlfriends and said, "See that guy down there? He looks like the kind of guy that is marriage material."

He was neat, looked well groomed and had a nice smile. Before I could count to ten, this guy was at my side. Our conversation flowed easily and before I knew it I gave him my phone number in New York. This man was very persistent. He called me over the next four days asking for a dinner date. I tried to put him off but agreed to have dinner with him on the fifth day before I planned to return home to San Francisco at the end of the week.

My girlfriends wanted to make sure that my dinner date was legitimate. They concocted a plan to remove his driver's license from his wallet to double check his identity. But when my date arrived at the all women's hotel where I was staying, he looked far from being a threat. My date was wearing a seersucker suit, a bow tie and dark glasses. He looked quite the catch, so the license scheme was dropped.

My date was terrific. He was genuinely nice, and had a great sense of humor. He immediately put me at ease until he escorted me into one of the most expensive restaurants in Manhattan. I wondered, *what does this guy want from me?*

The maitre'd escorted us to our table and presented me with a menu. To my shock, my menu had no prices. I now felt very uncomfortable. I kept remembering the phrase, *there is no such thing as a free lunch.* I firmly announced, "I really can't eat here. We have to go." So off to Longchamps we went where the prices didn't turn heads.

Our dinner date was fabulous. We talked easily to one another and never had a loss of things to say. We discovered that we both loved to dance. I agreed to meet him one more time before flying back to San Francisco.

Two nights later, he escorted me to the ultimate dance hall in New York City, the famous Rainbow Room, high above Rockefeller Center on Fifth Avenue. This art deco jewel of a building was the perfect backdrop for Swing Dancing and the Fox Trot. We danced until the wee hours of the night captivated by each other. Our bodies glided together so beautifully like it was "meant to be." Now I was wondering if I should go back to the West Coast or stay in New York. *Was this a one-week fling, or something with a future?*

I decided to keep my original plans and went back home. Within a few days of my return, Bruce started his campaign to get me to come back to New York by sending me two-dozen red roses. He was relentless and I slowly realized that I had some deep-seated feelings for him. After this realization, I made plans to move to New York to give this relationship a true test, rather than just carry on by long distance.

And as sure as the fates would have it, Bruce and I fell in love and decided to get married.

What was so remarkable about our meeting was the following revelation discovered when we each made our own guest list for the wedding. On my list I had a Richard Friedman, and Bruce listed a Rick Friedman. Could this be the same person? It turned out that we both knew the same guy but it had never come up in conversation. And do you remember the date that never happened…when the man cancelled his trip to SF because his flight sent him to L.A. instead? Yes, that was Bruce! I was the fix up that never happened!

Sylvia's Lesson

Follow your heart and your dreams may become a reality.

THE TEACHER AND THE TEACHER'S PET
ELLEN AND JOHN'S STORY

Ellen's Story

My parents were visiting and I was looking for an activity that might interest them. I heard that there was a lecture being given on the history of prominent San Francisco families. Since I was 28 and single, I thought this might give me a clue to understanding the genealogy of my city. I was dating a man, but he was more fun than marriage material. I always felt you can never have too many friends. My parents liked history so I signed the three of us up for this lecture.

We thoroughly enjoyed the presentation. My father wanted to meet the speaker and find out if he would consider traveling to Indianapolis to give a similar talk. Unbeknownst to me, the speaker asked if the young woman sitting next to him was his daughter, if I was married, and tried to wangle my name and phone number from my dad. Yes, John was successful and got the information he wanted.

The very next day John called to ask me out on a date. We found we had many similar likes and interests. Family was important. We had similar views on politics and world affairs. I enjoyed his company.

John's Story

Out of the corner of one eye I noticed a beautiful young woman sitting next to a man and woman who I suspected to be her parents. I thought to myself…*don't let her get away and try to find out who she is before this lecture ends.*

I was ready to start my lecture so any introductions would have to wait. Unabashed, I was able to interject the fact that I was 37 and single in my talk while looking directly at this lovely young face. After presenting and fielding questions from the audience, the man next to the beautiful young woman approached me at the lectern.

"We thoroughly enjoyed your program tonight. I was wondering if you ever travel out of town to give these kind of lectures to other groups?"

"Yes, periodically," I answered.

"Great," said the man from the audience. "May I please have your contact information?"

"Absolutely. And by the way, may I ask you a question? Is the beautiful young woman who was sitting next to you your daughter?"

"Yes, she is," he replied.

So with that introduction I was able to get Ellen's phone number.

I called her the very next day for a date. She was very gracious. After dinner I took her to the Top of the Mark, a hotel high on Nob Hill where you see the entire panorama of San Francisco glittering before your eyes. At that moment, I knew that this was the woman I was going to marry. She was gentle, sensitive, smart and had a great sense of humor.

I had to contain myself, with my new discovery of love. It would be a little forward to announce my intentions on a first date. So I waited.

Within a few days of our first date, I received a beautiful hand written note from Ellen thanking me for the wonderful time. I kept thinking, *how many women would write a guy a note like this?* She must like me.

I got up my courage and asked her out for coffee, our second date. We talked and talked. Somewhere at the end of the conversation I got up the courage and proposed… "Would you ever consider marrying me?"

To my relief she replied, "When you bring a ring we can discuss it."

The rest is history. I got the ring, she accepted and we are living happily ever after.

♥

Ellen and John's Lesson

Be open to the world around you.

EPILOGUE

Now that you have experienced the wonderful stories of *Chance Meetings That Tied the Knot,* I hope you will look at the world differently. A chance meeting lurks in every corner, at every crossroad, and at any time. One never knows when it will happen.

As these stories illustrate, chance meetings occur when you live an interesting and varied life. Try something new, explore, discover. Embrace the attitude that if it is meant to be, it will be! Just remember, one chance meeting can change your life, just as it did for me!

Jan Newman
Tea for Two

MY STORY

Name _____

Date _____

_____

_____

_____

_____

_____

_____

_____

_____

_____

_____

_____

_____

_____

_____

_____

My Story

Chance Meetings that Tied the Knot

My Story

♥

My Lesson Learned

_____

_____

_____

_____

_____

_____

_____

_____

_____

_____

_____

_____

_____

_____

_____

_____

_____

_____

_____

_____